The SEVEN SPIRITS *of* GOD

The Seven Spirits of God

Copyright 2021 © Brian Guerin

All rights reserved. No part of this book may be used or reproduced by any means, graphic, electronic, mechanical, including photocopying, recording, taping, or by any information storage retrieval system without the written permission of the author except in the case of brief quotations embodied in critical articles and reviews.

Unless otherwise noted, scriptures taken from the New King James Version®. Copyright © 1982 by Thomas Nelson. Used by permission. All rights reserved.

Scripture quotations from The Authorized (King James) Version. Rights in the Authorized Version in the United Kingdom are vested in the Crown. Reproduced by permission of the Crown's patentee, Cambridge University Press.

Scripture quotations marked (NLT) are taken from the Holy Bible, New Living Translation, copyright ©1996, 2004, 2015 by Tyndale House Foundation. Used by permission of Tyndale House Publishers, Carol Stream, Illinois 60188. All rights reserved.

ISBN: 9798533946476

*Cover design, typeset, & development by Tall Pine Books

*Published in the United States of America

The
SEVEN
SPIRITS
of GOD

Brian Guerin

CONTENTS

1. The Experiential Spirits... 7
2. The Menorah..17
3. The Spirit of Wisdom... 27
4. The Spirit of Understanding................................. 37
5. The Spirit of Counsel..49
6. The Spirit of Might.. 59
7. The Spirit of the Fear of the Lord....................... 67

    About the Author.. 79
    Free excerpt from to Know Him 81
    The Divine Door 83
    Intimacy's Value...91
    Experiential Knowledge...................................... 97
    Notes..105

I
THE EXPERIENTIAL SPIRITS

IT IS VITAL that the church experience the seven spirits of the Lord during the last hours in which we find ourselves. As we move closer to the coming of the Lord, we must be aware of what the seven spirits of God are and why we need them. We must understand the necessity of becoming a yielded company that walks in the fullness of the seven spirits, just as Jesus did.

In 2006, I had a dream about the Lord that was connected to an experience I would have fourteen years later. Both experiences were connected to awakening the last-day company, as we are being led into the end times. They were also tied into the seven spirits of God.

It was April 2006 when I had the first dream. As I entered into this experience, I found myself thrown into a three-year-long revival in the Spirit, in which I met William Seymour, historic founder of the Azusa

Street Revival. This revival occurred in Los Angeles beginning in 1906 and became one of the greatest mission movements in U.S. history. It just so happens that 2006 was its one-hundred-year anniversary. Those who experienced it spoke in new tongues as miracles regularly manifested in their midst. The Holy Spirit hit the revival so hard that as young missionaries spoke in their new tongues, they recognized which country they were being called to serve as missionaries due to the new languages they spoke.

In my dream, however, William Seymour was distraught. He looked at me and said, "Had I only known. I was just confused." He then turned to a slot machine beside him, pulled the lever, and watched as the numbers and fruit began to spin. I saw the numbers on the slot machine almost land on 777, and then I awoke. Upon waking, I felt the same way William did in my dream, distraught because I did not get to see the fullness of the 777. As I was trying to make sense of what had happened to me, the Holy Spirit spoke, saying, You were looking into His day and witnessing how close they were to seeing the completion of the seven spirits of God on a group of people. But your generation will see this completion.

Of the seven spirits of God, there were two spirits that were not present at the Azusa Street Revival. William told me that he did not know—which is reflective of the spirit of knowledge—and that he was confused—reflective of the spirit of understanding. God was showing me that when the seven spirits are out of balance, the enemy can find his way in. Revival cannot be sustained without all of the spirits of God. The Holy Spirit told me that in Seymour's day, they got close, but they could not see it; my generation will see it, however, it will lead to the culmination of all things—Jesus' return. The Azusa Street Revival diminished after three years because of this imbalance of the seven spirits of God.

Fourteen years after that dream, on Christmas Eve, my family and I were up late for the festivities. Shortly after we went to bed and fell asleep, I was awakened at 3:24 a.m. to an encounter of the hand of the Lord abruptly entering and hovering over my bed, knocking on a membrane over my room. I could see His knuckles hitting hard as I heard the heavy knocks multiple times. This was not a romantic or soft experience; it was stern and insistent. I have always known from experiences in my life that the knocking of the Lord is related to Revelation 3:20. It is very intimate and personal to me in a bridal way.

Knocking is in reference to the Laodicean church in the book of Revelation. If we hear His voice, we open the door and let Him dine with us. (See Revelation 3:20.) We are in the last generation before the return of the Lord. During the last Jubilee, I had a dream about the 144,000, indicating that we would have one last Jubilee before His return. No one knows the day or the hour, but people know the times and seasons. With that being said, we will be the last generation before the return of the Lord. The remedy to the last company is intimacy with the Lord. The church of Laodicea, the last church in the book of Revelation, represents our current generation. The last church's reward was to sit on the throne next to Him. But we must let Him in to dine with us.

Later, the Holy Spirit revealed to me that the knocking at 3:24 a.m. was in reference to Revelation 3:2–4, pertaining to the church of Sardis. But it was also in reference to the year 2024. The year 2020 was a shaking for the awakening that is to come. Those who are holding on to things that are shakable will feel it, but those who are ready for the awakening are holding on to the kingdom.

In Revelation, Jesus appeared and told John to write to the seven churches. To each church, Jesus appeared as the embodiment of something for a reason. He appeared to them to bring correction, and through it, to bring both redemption and a reward. But He displayed Himself in a unique way to each church in reference to their particular situation.

Be constantly alert, and strengthen the things that remain, which were about to die; for I have not found your deeds completed in the sight of My God.

> *So remember what you have received and heard; and keep it, and repent. Then if you are not alert, I will come like a thief, and you will not know at what hour I will come to you. But you have a few people in Sardis who have not soiled their garments; and they will walk with Me in white, for they are worthy. (Revelation 3:2–4)*

Verse 3 is very clear and carries a specific message for this generation: wake up! Jesus reveals himself to this church as the seven spirits. In my dream from 2006, the Lord was showing me an awakening that was diminished because of the lack of the seven spirits. All things connect to awakening and revival. The seven spirits of God are like a divine puzzle piece fabricated of the things of God.

> *Then the angel who had been speaking with me returned and woke me, like a person who is awakened from his sleep. (Zechariah 4:1)*

This was an awakening encounter that led right into the seven spirits of God. There is a shaking that leads to an awakening that many of us are crying out to experience. The Lord is wanting to produce a people yielded to and filled with the seven spirits of God. There will be a full people that resemble Jesus, no one lacking or weak. What is interesting about this encounter is that Zechariah was not actually asleep. It was only as if he were asleep. This encounter initiated his awakening experience.

> *And he said to me, "What do you see?" And I said, "I see, and behold, a lampstand all of gold with its bowl on the top of it, and its seven lamps on it with seven spouts belonging to each of the lamps which are on the top of it; also two olive trees by it, one on the right side of the bowl and the other on its left side." Then I said to the angel who was speaking with me, saying, "What are these, my Lord?" So the angel who was speaking with me answered and said to me, "Do you not know what these are?" And I said, "No, my Lord." Then he said to me, "This is the word of the Lord to Zerubbabel, saying, 'Not by might nor by power, but by My Spirit,' says the Lord of armies. 'What are you, you great mountain? Before Zerubbabel you will become a plain; and he will bring out the top stone with shouts of "Grace, grace to it!"'" Also the word of the Lord came to me, saying, "The hands of Zerubbabel have laid the foundation of this house, and his hands will finish it. Then you will know that the Lord of armies has sent me to you. For who has shown contempt for the day of small things? But these seven will rejoice when they see the plumb line in the hand of Zerubbabel—*

they are the eyes of the Lord roaming throughout the earth." (verses 2–10)

This was the last prophetic temple imagery in the Old Testament. There was Moses' temple, David's tent and Solomon's temple—places to worship God. In the New Testament, we understand that we are the temple housing the Spirit of God. This imagery in Zechariah is a projection of how we should be as a temple.

We see that olive trees are important to this Scripture. The two olive trees are next to a bowl, which represents God. The trees produce olive oil that runs into the bowl through tubes, and then the bowl feeds the seven lamps, keeping them continually burning. The trees are the two witnesses in Revelation, and the seven lamps are the seven spirits of the Lord.

John to the seven churches that are in Asia: Grace to you and peace from Him who is, and who was, and who is to come, and from the seven spirits who are before His throne, and from Jesus Christ, the faithful witness, the firstborn of the dead, and the ruler of the kings of the earth. To Him who loves us and released us from our sins by His blood. (Revelation 1:4–5)

Out from the throne came flashes of lightning and sounds and peals of thunder. And there were seven

> lamps of fire burning before the throne, which are the seven spirits of God. (Revelation 4:5)

> And I saw between the throne (with the four living creatures) and the elders a Lamb standing, as if slaughtered, having seven horns and seven eyes, which are the seven spirits of God sent out into all the earth. (Revelation 5:6)

Notice, the only description of the lamb is tied to the end-time seals. This leads to the end-time seals being opened. Our depiction of Jesus is "slaughtered," as a lamb. This lamb is displayed as having the seven spirits of God. The seven spirits, and the fullness of them, will be upon the company just as they were upon Jesus. The two olive trees are projections of the Lord's return. It is an end-times model that will sustain and keep the seven spirits burning bright. It will enable a move of the Spirit that will sustain until the Lord's return, which we see depicted in Revelation. The olive trees are constantly keeping the seven spirits of the Lord lit.

> Then there was given to me, a measuring rod like a staff; and someone said, "Get up and measure the temple of God and the altar, and those who worship in it. Leave out the courtyard which is outside the temple and do not measure it, because it has been given to the nations; and they will trample the holy

city for forty-two months. And I will grant authority to my two witnesses, and they will prophesy for 1,260 days, clothed in sackcloth." These are the two olive trees and the two lampstands that stand before the Lord of the earth. And if anyone wants to harm them, fire flows out of their mouth and devours their enemies; and so if anyone wants to harm them, he must be killed in this way. These have the power to shut up the sky, so that rain will not fall during the days of their prophesying; and they have power over the waters to turn them into blood, and to strike the earth with every plague, as often as they desire. When they have finished their testimony, the beast that comes up out of the abyss will make war with them, and overcome them and kill them. And their dead bodies will lie on the street of the great city which spiritually is called Sodom and Egypt, where also their Lord was crucified. Those from the peoples, tribes, languages, and nations will look at their dead bodies for three and a half days, and will not allow their dead bodies to be laid in a tomb. And those who live on the earth will rejoice over them and celebrate; and they will send gifts to one another, because these two prophets tormented those who live on the earth. And after the three and a half days, the breath of life from God came into them, and they stood on their feet; and great fear fell upon those who were watching them. And they heard a loud voice from heaven saying to them, "Come up here." And they went up into heaven in the cloud, and their enemies watched them. And at that time there was a great earthquake, and a tenth of the city fell; seven thousand people were killed in the earthquake, and the rest were terrified and gave glory to the God of heaven. (Revelation 11:1–13)

Immediately after these verses, the last trumpet is blown and the Lord returns. The two witnesses in Zechariah are connected to the seven spirits of God. Jesus opening the scroll and the seals are representative of the seven spirits of God. The two witnesses are first seen in Zechariah, ministering to the Lord through the oil of the olive trees. The oil (our intimacy with the Lord) goes first, supplying the bowl (God). The bowl then fills the seven lampstands (the seven spirits of God), which releases His governance. This is the Holy Spirit, maxed out like the bridegroom leading to the marriage supper of the lamb. When you start looking in depth at the seven spirits of God, you see that it is absolutely imperative that the last company walk in them. The final hour is not a time to be dogmatic about your biblical or Christian lens, limiting the capacity to which you walk with God and in the Spirit.

2
THE MENORAH

Then you shall make a lampstand of pure gold. The lampstand, its base and its shaft, are to be made of hammered work; its cups, its bulbs, and its flowers shall be of one piece with it. Six branches shall go out from its sides; three branches of the lampstand from its one side and three branches of the lampstand from its other side. Three cups shall be shaped like almond blossoms on the one branch, a bulb and a flower, and three cups shaped like almond blossoms on the other branch, a bulb and a flower—the same for six branches going out from the lampstand; and on the lampstand four cups shaped like almond blossoms, its bulbs and its flowers. A bulb shall be under the first pair of branches coming out of it, and a bulb under the second pair of branches coming out of it, and a bulb under the third pair of branches

> coming out of it, for the six branches coming out of the lampstand. Their bulbs and their branches shall be of one piece with it; all of it shall be one piece of hammered work of pure gold. Then you shall make its lamps seven in number; and they shall mount its lamps so as to shed light on the space in front of it. Its tongs and its trays shall be of pure gold. It shall be made from a talent of pure gold, with all these utensils. See that you make them by the pattern for them, which was shown to you on the mountain. (Exodus 25:31-40)

THE MENORAH WAS first constructed by Moses to reflect the blueprint of heaven, taken from the exact design God gave him. It is also meant to represent the seven spirits continually burning before the throne in the temple. It is one of the most symbolic representations of the seven spirits of God.

As described in the Bible, the menorah is a seven-flamed lampstand made of pure gold (anything near glory was covered in gold), used in the tabernacle erected in the wilderness by Moses and then later in the temple in Jerusalem. Fresh olive oil of the purest quality was used daily to burn its lamps. The two olive trees are representative of the two witnesses in Revelation 11. They supply the bowl with oil that feeds the seven lamps. Your intimate relationship is the supply that keeps the seven spirits lit. It is one of the models in

Scripture that seems backward. Our adoration is what presses the oil into God and trickles into the seven spirits, which are then released within us. When breaking down the seven spirits, we see that each spirit is introduced with —*the spirit of*.... The word *spirit* in this introduction can be literally translated as *the breath of God.*

In the description of how the menorah was to be created, God told Moses to hammer out the base and shaft before anything else. The base and shaft are representative of *intimacy*. Just as the vertical beam of the cross points to heaven as a symbol of vertical intimacy with God, the menorah does the same. The spirits of God emerge out of the *base* and *shaft* of the menorah. Wisdom, understanding, counsel, might, knowledge and the fear of the Lord only come from intimacy with Jesus.

The *branches* of the menorah are the lamps of the seven spirits. We read above that each branch is to have three golden almond flowers, except for the base, which has four. The root word for *almond* means "to watch or wake." The almonds are symbolic of *watching* for an *awakening*. Almond trees are the first trees to awaken from winter and the first of Israel's trees to bloom. There is a rapid watching that is meant for us to see what the Lord is doing. These almond flowers project the Lord watching His people. He is fervently waiting for the awakening so He can be in complete unity with us.

Nearest to the throne of God, the closest one can be to the Lord in proximity, are the *four* living creatures, each with four faces. Of all the things God could have chosen to be closest to Him, he picked these four. Similarly, there are four almond flowers on the base and main shaft of the menorah, an exemplification of where they are in reference to our unity with God.

> *Then a shoot will spring from the stem of Jesse, and a Branch from his roots will bear fruit. The Spirit of the Lord will rest on Him, the spirit of wisdom and understanding, the spirit of counsel and strength, the spirit of knowledge and the fear of the Lord. (Isaiah 11:1–2)*

The Spirit of the Lord is the base, out of which wisdom, understanding, counsel, strength, knowledge and the fear of the Lord emerge. This is the clearest description of what the seven spirits' functions are and is connected to the Spirit Jesus walked in while on earth. We never see the seven spirits apart from Jesus. The seven spirits are directly linked to each of the lamps on the menorah. There is a precise counterbalance regarding the position of the seven spirits of God in accordance with the menorah. It is almost as if there is a single branch connecting them on the menorah. The coupled spirits of God are dependent on each other, meaning you will never see one without the other. God did this on purpose to ensure that things must act dependently on one another, like a husband and wife or a bride and bridegroom. Because of this, it is imperative that none of the flames ever go out. When one flame goes out, it affects the connecting flame. If one of the seven spirits goes out, an imbalance is created, and a lack of function in the connected spirit. Jesus always sent out the disciples in twos. God's model breathes dependency because we *need* each other.

COUPLED BRANCHES

> *Blessed is a person who finds wisdom, and one who obtains understanding. ...The* Lord *founded the earth by wisdom, He established the heavens by understanding. ...The beginning of wisdom is: acquire wisdom; and with all your possessions, acquire understanding. ...Does not wisdom call, and understanding raises her voice? ...On the lips of the discerning, wisdom is found, but a rod is for the back of him who has no sense. ...Wisdom rests in the heart of one who has understanding, but among fools it is made known. ...How much better it is to get wisdom than gold! And to get understanding is to be chosen above silver. (Proverbs 3:13, 19, 4:7, 8:1, 10:13, 14:33, 16:16)*

Wisdom is with the aged, and with long life comes understanding. (Job 12:12)

Wisdom and understanding are often coupled in Scripture. They are always mentioned with one another, making a point to show how dependent they are on one another. Understanding is pointless without wisdom, and wisdom without understanding does not exist. There is need for balance all throughout Scripture, balancing wisdom and understanding, not in a religious context but in the fullness of what the Lord has for us. If we are not careful, we can become imbalanced by prioritizing one thing over another. When this happens, our intimacy with the Lord can become compromised by allowing imbalances that affect how we live.

In looking at the different aspects, or attributes, of the seven spirits of God, it is absolutely imperative to realize the substance of who He is as the driving force and sustaining source behind each of them. They are God-infused aspects of His nature, meant to be always in operation through His bride. Jesus is the highest model. If He was able to walk in them, we can do so as well. He desires us, created in His image, to reflect His nature, which is also the seven spirits.

There are no natural limitations or connections to mere human wisdom, knowledge, understanding or counsel. When we talk about "the spirit of," we are superseding the natural limitations of man on every front. That is why the last-hour company will stand out as a reflection of the Bridegroom like no one else. The Spirit of God is rushing through the seven spirits, and if you have them in you, you will stand out as the bride of Christ. The breath, wind or spirit, in and through you, is the spirit of wisdom. Remain full of the Holy Spirit, that you may flow through the spirit that God has available to you. It is also worth mentioning that that these seven spirits are different from the gifts of the Spirit. While both are vital and biblical, they are different applications in the expression of God. This does not mean the gifts are not important, because they are very important and meaningful to our lives. They are just different. We want both; it is not either/or. There is a gift of wisdom we can tap into for ourselves or for others, but the *spirit of wisdom* is God's wisdom. When we walk through the spirit of wisdom, it never leaves us.

I once experienced a spiritual encounter in which I was locked into praying in tongues. I saw the Lord walking toward me, but His appearance was *all light*. He came closer and closer, full of power and might as the resurrected Lord. As He approached, I had a random thought: *if a friend of mine could see the Lord this way, they would be amazed.* I was in such a deep place of glory that my small, random thought was heard by God. The next morning, my friend called and told me that they had a dream in which the Lord approached them in all light and power. The spiritual encounter I had experienced triggered a similar experience for my friend!

When you are in a deep place of His presence, you do not even have to ask; you think and the Lord hears, unlocking the realm of the Spirit. When you are in His creative nature, the thoughts you have will matter to God. When you are in the deep presence of the Lord, ask, even when you are lost in your intimacy with Him. The deeper you are, the less physical asking is needed. Be so close to Him that He will clearly hear your slightest whisper.

After I saw the Lord in my vision, I also saw a sword touch my shoulder to knight me and a goblet, both of which I understood as being signs of wisdom and understanding. Then the Lord gave me three wishes, asking what I wanted from Him. The first thing I asked for was to be able to love Him as no one else has ever loved Him. Second, I asked to be able to obey Him unlike anyone else has ever obeyed Him. I was in such a deep visionary place that these things left my mouth before I could even think about what I was saying. Then I stopped for a moment on my third wish, knowing it was my last. It occurred to me that the only one whom God had ever asked what they wanted was Solomon. The one thing Solomon asked for was wisdom, and because of that, he acquired great understanding, wealth and governance. So, I also asked for wisdom. My natural response, considering my Bible college background, very well could have been to ask for power, glory or miracles. But as I have studied more deeply about the last-day bride, I have discovered that wisdom, understanding, knowledge and counsel are being overlooked and will eventually become as valuable as gold.

We want the seven-fold spirit of God to possess us so much that His governance will flow out of us constantly. You may not be at all educated, but if the spirit of wisdom falls upon you, you will be ahead in the destiny that God has for you. Solomon had the spirit of wisdom, not just the gift. By the wisdom of God, Solomon knew how to resolve the issue of the two women who were fighting over the child.

> *Then the king said, "The one says, 'This is my son who is living, and your son is the dead one'; and the other says, 'No! For your son is the dead one, and my son is the living one.'" And the king said, "Get me a sword." So they brought a sword before the king. And the king said, "Cut the living child in two, and give half to the one and half to the other." But the woman whose child was the living one spoke to the king, for she was deeply stirred over her son, and she said, "Pardon me, my lord! Give her the living child, and by no means kill him!" But the other woman was saying, "He shall be neither mine nor yours; cut him!" Then the king replied, "Give the first woman the living child, and by no means kill him. She is his mother." When all Israel heard about the judgment which the king had handed down, they feared the*

king, because they saw that the wisdom of God was in him to administer justice. (1 Kings 3:23–28)

Solomon was acting in the spirit of Wisdom, not just in his earthly wisdom. His earthly wisdom may have made a decision that seemed justified at the time but could have ended badly. God's wisdom will always be the right answer.

For the foolishness of God is wiser than mankind, and the weakness of God is stronger than mankind. (1 Corinthians 1:25)

Without intimacy, the flames will not stay lit, and there could be a weak link in your chain that provides the enemy an availability to exploit. We need to be vigilant and aware of the seven spirits so that we are not missing anything, specifically wisdom and understanding. We want a revival that will be sustained and not die because of lack in the Spirit of God.

3
THE SPIRIT OF WISDOM

THE SPIRIT OF wisdom is God's capacity to judging *rightly* in matters relating to life and conduct. It is the soundness of judgement in the choice of means and ends.

> *The Son of Man came eating and drinking, and they say, "Behold, a gluttonous man and a heavy drinker, a friend of tax collectors and sinners!" And yet wisdom is vindicated by her deeds. (Matthew 11:19)*

Wisdom is not skeptical, cynical or accusative. Never be judgmental in your wisdom, because it becomes distasteful to the Holy Spirit and does not show the love of Jesus. Wisdom must be enforced with love, and love trusts all things. In the verse above, Jesus is essentially saying that wisdom is known by its results. When true wisdom is present, it will prove itself by its fruit. We can have great human wisdom but if we lack in God's wisdom, there will never be fruit to back it up. The proof, as they say, is in the pudding. A healthy way of identifying whether wisdom is coming from the Lord is by examining the fruit in the life of the person spouting that wisdom. If someone is following the wisdom of God, then fruit will naturally follow it. *"Wisdom is vindicated by her deeds."* There may be words that people consider to be wisdom, but nothing will indicate it being from the Lord.

Knowledge is mandatory and vital when operating in the seven spirits, but alone, knowledge will not produce worthy fruit. Wisdom *with* knowledge produces Godly fruit.

When my son played basketball, I saw different coaches come and go. Some of them were highly intelligent with a lot of knowledge but they lacked wisdom. For instance, one of his coaches was able to go through the team's strategies from memory and had the players out their plays before the game began. But he lacked wisdom, because by acting out the plays on the court, he revealed the team's strategies to the other team's coaches. High intellect does not mean high wisdom. Wisdom is the *soundness* of judgement.

Wisdom is imperative in reference to building something. In the Spirit, this means being apostolic.

Wisdom is greatly needed when building anything. It ensures that what you are building will not collapse.

By wisdom a house is built, and by understanding it is established; and by knowledge the rooms are filled. (Proverbs 24:3–4)

Then I was beside Him, as a master workman; and I was His delight daily, rejoicing always before Him. (Proverbs 8:30)

The wise woman builds her house, but the foolish tears it down with her own hands. (Proverbs 14:1)

The LORD founded the earth by wisdom, He established the heavens by understanding. (Proverbs 3:19)

The context of building can be applied to many different things in life. For instance, it applies to family life, business, personal growth, spiritual growth, relational growth and ministry. When the wisdom of God combines with the knowledge you have acquired in areas of your life, they become like a well-oiled machine. Knowledge can water the flowerbed, but wisdom pulls the weeds. You can apply wisdom to your knowledge in each of these areas of your life. If you desire wisdom, ask God and He will give it to you generously!

> *But if any of you lacks wisdom, let him ask of God, who gives to all generously and without reproach, and it will be given to him. (James 1:5)*

Big decisions come often in life. When we are depending solely on our own wisdom, we will have a hard time making a choice that is remotely successful, but when we operate out of God's wisdom, we will always be successful. We should never operate out of our own wisdom. You have a wellspring of wisdom from the Holy Spirit residing within you—you need to use it! Dig into the well of wisdom, understanding and knowledge that lies within you.

When you are in deep intimacy with Jesus, you can clearly see the importance of digging down into the well of the Holy Spirit. Intimacy brings clarity. When you are lacking in that intimacy, the light in the lamps of the seven spirits may dim, obscuring what is Godly wisdom and what is earthly wisdom. When you are lacking wisdom, you may try to dip into the wellspring, but nothing comes up. Intimacy is everything when growing in the seven spirits.

After these things Jesus was walking in Galilee, for He was unwilling to walk in Judea because the Jews were seeking to kill Him. Now the feast of the Jews, the Feast of Booths, was near. So His brothers said to Him, "Move on from here and go into Judea, so that Your disciples also may see Your works which You are doing.

For no one does anything in secret when he himself is striving to be known publicly. If You are doing these things, show Yourself to the world." For not even His brothers believed in Him. So Jesus said to them, "My time is not yet here, but your time is always ready. The world cannot hate you, but it hates Me because I testify about it, that its deeds are evil. Go up to the feast yourselves; I am not going up to this feast, because my time has not yet fully arrived." Now having said these things to them, He stayed in Galilee. (John 7:1–9)

Jesus applied wisdom to a situation that could have had an enormously negative impact on His ministry. It was not His time to reveal to the world the fact that He was Christ, but His brothers wanted Him to do so. He could have applied His brothers' earthly wisdom and done what they were asking Him to do, but instead, Jesus obeyed the Holy Spirit and used the spirit of wisdom.

These verses also reveal that as the days edge closer to the end times, the kingdom of light will only become brighter and purer, while the kingdom of darkness will become darker and more forceful. There will be a collision between them that will be unmistakable.

For over a decade, I built custom homes with my dad. The Lord reminded me that we used to work with a lot of different high-end architects and interior designers. These architects had to complete a lot of education and do a lot of research to get where they were. There were so many different logistics and building codes they had to follow. Sometimes, bigger homes would become so complex that the roof lines were too complicated for them to compute in their heads. In these instances, they would put V.O.J. on the blueprints, meaning *verify on the job*. These complicated figures and problems were then put on us builders. We had to take the knowledge of the situation and apply wisdom, judging rightly so we could complete the construction.

Wisdom must have knowledge, but knowledge alone doesn't cut it.

> *Riches and honor are with me [wisdom], enduring wealth and righteousness. (Proverbs 8:18)*

> *To endow those who love me [wisdom] with wealth, that I may fill their treasuries. (Proverbs 8:21)*

Solomon wrote these proverbs. He was the wisest man to ever live but he was also the wealthiest. In today's terms, his wealth would add up to $2.5 trillion. No one today is even close to having that amount of wealth. But God's wisest man was wealthy beyond imagination. Wealth is always attributed to wisdom.

> *The reward of humility and the fear of the Lord are riches, honor, and life. (Proverbs 22:4)*

Wherever there is a healthy dose of arrogance or pride, wisdom is nowhere to be found. When you see arrogance and pride in someone, they are far from the wisdom of God. This also has to do with *yielding yourself* to Jesus so you can work through the seven spirits. Humility and wisdom are best friends.

The reward of humility and the fear of the Lord are riches, honor, and life. (Proverbs 11:2)

Humility and wisdom attract each other. Wealth is a side effect of being humble and walking in God's wisdom.

The fear of the Lord is to hate evil; pride, arrogance, the evil way, and the perverted mouth, I hate. (Proverbs 8:13)

There are people without the wisdom of God who are meant to be leaders of their generation. But the enemy has picked them off for his use. You can tell when someone has a call on their life, but instead, they waste their life on darkness.

God still has a plan for them and their influential lives. Leading in natural wisdom with arrogance, their fruit will be dead on the vine and their teachings will be earthly.

The wise of heart will receive commands, but a babbling fool will come to ruin. (Proverbs 10:8)

When there are many words, wrongdoing is unavoidable, but one who restrains his lips is wise. (Proverbs 10:19)

Blessed is the person who listens to me [wisdom], watching daily at my gates, waiting at my doorposts. (Proverbs 8:34)

The way of a fool is right in his own eyes, but a person who listens to advice is wise. (Proverbs 12:15)

Great listeners are always attributed to wisdom. If you can open your ears and step past pride, you will learn what is best for you or others in confusing situations. Being a good listener means admitting you don't have all the answers and being willing to submit to what the Lord has for you.

Often, we have the knowledge to get by in certain situations, but we don't have the wisdom of God. We do not want to simply walk in our own wisdom and "get by"; we want to walk in the Lord's wisdom so we can flourish. We want our personal spirits to be overtaken by the Holy Spirit. We want the spirit of wisdom to answer before our own wisdom even attempts to take over. We desire for the Lord's perfect ways, not our own earthly ways that can cause problems. The spirit of wisdom can make an enormous difference in your day-to-day life. The spirit of wisdom will keep knowledge applicable in the most productive and rightly provided ways.

4

THE SPIRIT OF UNDERSTANDING

IN MY VISION of William Seymour, the second spirit of God he said was lacking was the spirit of understanding.

The Hebrew terminology for understanding means "clear consideration and discernment." The root word for the term understanding means "to stand under something or have discernment of something." When you "stand under" something, you are at its foundation—familiar with it front to back. Understanding has a great depth of familiarity with the Spirit of God, but it is also to stand in the midst of or in between. Understanding brings you under the presence of God and His spirits.

And one of the elders said to me, "Stop weeping; behold, the Lion that is from the tribe of Judah, the Root of David, has overcome so as to open the book and its seven seals." And I saw between the throne (with the four living creatures) and the elders a Lamb standing, as if slaughtered, having seven horns and seven eyes, which are the seven spirits of God sent out into all the earth. (Revelation 5:5–6)

Here, we see Jesus, the Lamb slain, getting ready to break the seven seals. One of the main depictions of the Lamb is that He has the seven spirits of God. He is slain but the only other depiction of Him in the last hour is that He works through the seven spirits. The seven spirits come on the scene with great emphasis in the last hour. If Jesus is portraying and emphasizing what He is like, we should follow and become like Him in that way. The seven spirits of God must be fully lit, like the menorah, with their brightness showing upon Jesus. In between the throne and where the four creatures sat stood the Lamb slain, with seven eyes and horns—the seven spirits. Revelation, Ezekiel and Isaiah all mention the Father on the throne, with the four living creatures around the throne. Beyond them is another group, the twenty-four elders. In the center of all of them is Jesus. The four living creatures work in tandem with Jesus to open the seals because they have understanding. They stood in the midst of Jesus, which is what understanding means.

Jesus opens the first seal, and one of the four creatures responds when Jesus tells him to come and the white horse is loosed. The creatures have understanding of the situation because they are in proximity to Him who has all understanding. You do not want to be outside of the place where Jesus is—in the Holy of Holies. You can be born again outside of it, in the courts, but you may not receive the spirit of understanding until you reach the Holy of Holies. You must stand under and be in the midst of Jesus. If you want to work step-by-step with Jesus in His power and glory, you need the spirit of understanding.

When Jesus breaks the second seal in Revelation, the next of the four living creatures says to Him, "come." This goes on from seal to creature, revealing practical wisdom of what understanding is: being in His midst, receiving the understanding He is giving.

The Spirit of the Lord will rest on Him, the spirit of wisdom and understanding, the spirit of counsel and strength, the spirit of knowledge and the fear of the Lord. (Isaiah 11:2)

Imagine you are counseling a husband and wife. To be able to come to a point of understanding, you must stand in the midst of or between them. If you start hearing one side over another, you cannot have understanding in the situation.

This is where we want to be at all times regarding the things and the voice of God, with the spirit of understanding burning bright. It is also important to know that understanding is current and constant. The spirit of understanding may seem simple or small, but it is vital. The -ing in understanding keeps it "in the moment" at all times. It is not to be understood or to merely understand at a given point but rather, understanding is continual. It is not an isolated gift in the moment. The spirit of understanding is always moving. You are meant to grasp its meaning. It's to be thoroughly aware of or to have expertise in the meaning of something. It means that you understand it, through and through. God's understanding supersedes any kind of understanding of man.

Understanding is vital in these last hours, and in the days ahead. We all must have a grasp on the spirit of understanding. Confusion is a lack of understanding and is not of God. This generation can sense that we are in the times and seasons of the last days. I travel a lot, and what I hear from people all over the world is the same: the signs of the times are happening now. And although the spirit of understanding was lacking in generations prior, our generation will need it to finish the race. Scripture is clear that during the end times, deception will be at an all-time high. Deception is the exact opposing force to understanding. Doctrines of demons and people straying from the truth are going to be ever-increasing at unprecedented levels. With the spirit of understanding, we can cut through that deception like a razor. Deception can be thick like the foggiest day you can imagine, but those who are burning bright with the seven spirits will see right through it.

For the time will come when they will not tolerate sound doctrine; but wanting to have their ears tickled, they will accumulate for themselves teachers in accordance with their own desires, and they will turn their ears away from the truth and will turn aside to myths. (2 Timothy 4:3–4)

Now more than ever, you need to devour the words of the Bible. Read every day and teach your children to read Scripture every day as well. Fall madly in love with the Word of God, reading it front to back and getting your hands on any material you need to gain better understanding about His Word. Dig your heels deep into the living, God-breathed joyful and wise words of God. The Bible is a physical form of Jesus that you can take part in every day. So do not sleep on Him and His words. There is a current with a demonic anointing that is weaving itself into the world, making people question the legitimacy of Scripture. Be vigilant and mindful of this and seek out His wisdom and understanding on your own.

But the Spirit explicitly says that in later times some will fall away from the faith, paying attention to deceitful spirits and teachings of demons, by means of the hypocrisy of liars seared in their own conscience as with a branding iron. (1 Timothy 4:1–2)

In 2011, I was in prayer and had a vision of a blue principality. It was a giant, blue demonic-looking figure that put the Hulk to shame. This creature was opening a gate to hell. As it did, it released blue snakes onto the earth. After it released the snakes, it threw its head back and laughed in a wicked tone. Events from that year revealed to me what this vision had been referencing. Blue is the color of Revelation, and that gate released doctrines of demons. The color brings the false belief that what these demons are teaching is revelatory and from God, but instead, it is from the pits of hell.

During 2011, hyper-grace teaching came onto the scene in the church, as doctrines promoting the belief that hell doesn't exist became prevalent. These are unbiblical teachings that do not reflect the Lord or the Bible. That is why we must be in the Bible for ourselves, so we do not get caught up in deceptions of demons. Deception is one of the most frequently used arrows the enemy pulls out of his demonic quiver. It is also the most effective way to challenge humanity's understanding. When the flame of understanding is burning bright, the devil's arrows become like plastic that burns up in the fire. Those without the flame of understanding may be hit by the enemy's arrows that go in deep.

This is how so many false movements that use Scriptures deceptively begin.

In 2020, I had a dream of a religious movement I had been unaware of that had gained popularity. The core beliefs of this movement were tied to a verse in 1 Samuel:

For rebellion is as reprehensible as the sin of divination, and insubordination is as reprehensible as false religion and idolatry. (1 Samuel 15:23)

This movement is tied to rebellion, which is witchcraft. We must watch with the understanding of God so we can catch on to the deception of the enemy. The understanding of man will easily fall for the deception of the enemy. Some people have knowledge but lack the understanding of God. You can have incredible amounts of knowledge, but when the knowledge you do have is void of understanding, by default, it turns into deception. That is why knowledge and understanding need to be taken seriously. There must be balance in all seven of the spirits of God. We must operate in the full government of God. Wisdom and understanding are what keep the scales of knowledge balanced. The enemy is content with you having knowledge alone, but he is not okay with you having wisdom or understanding with that knowledge. If there is no knowledge, then wisdom and understanding are not even an option.

We know that we all have knowledge. Knowledge makes one conceited, but love edifies people. (1 Corinthians 8:1)

Being darkened in their understanding, excluded from the life of God because of the ignorance that is in them, because of the hardness of their heart; and they, having become callous, have given themselves up to indecent behavior for the practice of every kind of impurity with greediness. (Ephesians 4:18–19)

Give me understanding, so that I may comply with Your Law and keep it with all my heart. (Psalm 119:34)

The spirit of understanding illuminates the Word of God. It illuminates His voice, presence, ways and direction. The fullness of the life of God is attributed to those who have the spirit of understanding.

At the end of ten days their appearance seemed better and they were fatter than all the youths who had been eating the king's choice food. So the overseer continued to withhold their choice food and the wine they were to drink, and kept giving them vegetables. As for these four youths, God gave them knowledge and intelligence in every branch of literature and wisdom; Daniel even understood all kinds of visions and dreams. Then at the end of the days which the king had specified for presenting them, the commander of the officials presented them before Nebuchadnezzar. The king talked with them, and out of them all not one was found like Daniel, Hananiah, Mishael and Azariah; so they entered the king's personal service. As for every matter of wisdom and understanding about which the king consulted them, he found them ten times better than all the magicians and conjurers who were in all his realm. And Daniel continued until the first year of Cyrus the king. (Daniel 1:15–21 nasb95)

Understanding is attached to Daniel's fasting. If you are desiring more wisdom and understanding, do the Daniel fast and seek the Lord. Daniel and the others were ten times better in every way than anyone else because of the wisdom and understanding that came from fasting. Daniel is a great example of the power of God on His people when they operate in the spirits of wisdom and understanding.

In the third year of Cyrus king of Persia a message was revealed to Daniel, who was named Belteshazzar; and the message was true and one of great conflict, but he understood the message and had an understanding of the vision. (Daniel 10:1 nasb95)

In the verse above, Daniel experienced a vision and immediately had understanding about the vision. There are many times when the idea of understanding is associated with Daniel. The Daniel fast, accompanied with prayer, will unlock understanding like nothing else. Typically, when the Lord is calling or leading you into a Daniel fast, He is desiring to take you into greater understanding in order to further develop the purpose and call He has for you on earth.

> *So then, be careful how you walk, not as unwise people but as wise, making the most of your time, because the days are evil. Therefore do not be foolish, but understand what the will of the Lord is. And do not get drunk with wine, in which there is debauchery, but be filled with the Spirit. (Ephesians 5:15–18)*

> *For this reason we also, since the day we heard about it, have not ceased praying for you and asking that you may be filled with the knowledge of His will in all spiritual wisdom and understanding, so that you will walk in a manner worthy of the Lord, to please Him in all respects, bearing fruit in every good work and increasing in the knowledge of God. (Colossians 1:9–10)*

You will not be afraid of the terror by night, or of the arrow that flies by day; of the plague that stalks in darkness, or of the destruction that devastates at noon. (Psalm 91:5–6)

You will not live a life worthy of the Lord, pleasing Him in every way and burning brightly in the last days, if you are devoid of the spirit of wisdom and understanding. In this last hour, understanding will be more valuable than gold, silver, rubies or anything else of substantial value. People with understanding see clearly and are not easily deceived. They do not fall prey to the enemy's number one plan of attack: deception. "The arrow that flies by day" in Psalm 91 is often a deceptive arrow.

The danger of deception is that when you are deceived, you do not realize that you are being deceived. In these last days, there will be more and more arrows of deception coming at us. If we are not hiding in the shadow of the Almighty, staying in the secret place of deep intimacy, those arrows will hit us and understanding will leave us completely. Gain the spirit of understanding!

5
THE SPIRIT OF COUNSEL

MANY OF US, by nature, want to focus on the virtues of who we are, the substance of what we carry or who we can connect with to add more capability to the things we do. We see clearly that heaven's design is typically fueled by the revelation that embodies wisdom, understanding, knowledge and counsel. The revelatory realm is absolutely imperative.

In American football, a running back needs to be fast and strong to run the ball. Even so, if he doesn't also have wisdom and knowledge regarding the plays and schemes of the game, he will never succeed. A person who inherits a large sum of money may immediately find themselves in a position of strength in the financial realm, but if they have no understanding and wisdom about the proper tools and methods of saving and investing, that person will likely be broke within a few years.

The Hebrew word for counsel means "advice, design, strategize, scheme and the consultation of God." The strategy of Heaven is God's counsel in any given moment. Thank God this is available to us because it is absolutely vital in the last hour. The spirit of counsel is Joshua walking around the city of Jericho seven times. For the walls to fall down, Joshua had to have the counsel of the Lord. This is where knowledge, wisdom and understanding do not complete the recipe by themselves.

There have been many people who have had downloads from the spirit of counsel but later, stepped out of their deep intimacy with God. Later in life, when they tried to apply the counsel from those prior seasons, it was no longer applicable to the times. There's a reason why Joshua never attempted to walk around a city seven times ever again. That counsel came for a particular moment, and in a deep intimate place meant for that time. I love this about the attributes of the Holy Spirit, that He is consistent but does not allow for lack when others try to take credit for His work. That is why people like Joshua and David were so successful. Even after their successes, they continued to consult the Lord to get the current counsel or strategy of God. They leaned deeply into the spirit of counsel. They would not budge or try to implement their own ideas. They wanted the counsel of God, and God only. If you receive direction in the spirit of counsel, the counsel that is birthed out of it will not be shaken. It does not play by the world's rules at all. The spirit of counsel is the most stable thing you can have, even when everything else is being shaken.

There is a shaking going on all over the world. Right now, as things are being shaken, if you do not have your decision making rooted in the spirit of counsel, you will not be successful. Not because you are being unbiblical or not submitting the will of the Lord, but because you are not in the spirit of counsel. There is a great saying: "It is a good idea but not a God idea." God's ideas are what will keep us from falling when the shaking occurs.

> *For a Child will be born to us, a Son will be given to us; and the government will rest on His shoulders; and His name will be called Wonderful Counselor, Mighty God, Eternal Father, Prince of Peace. (Isaiah 9:6)*

In this verse, we see that counsel and might are connected. They are also connected on their two branches of the menorah. Might is the vehicle that drives counsel home. They are both needed but they also need each other. God is mighty and counseling. No one who flows in the apostolic gifts will be lacking in the spirit of counsel. There may be people who have counsel and insight on the Word or on relational healing, but if they do not have the spirit of counsel, they are working from their own might. If the flames are not fueled by intimacy, they will be unbalanced. Old wine doesn't pour out of the new counsel of God. There are times when believers become frustrated and begin to rebuke the devil, but the enemy is nowhere to be seen because God is saying, "That is not My current counsel." The Spirit is the substance of Him, unlike the gifts of the Spirit. We must be in the continual Spirit of God.

> *Now when the Philistines heard that they had anointed David king over Israel, all the Philistines went up to seek out David; and when David heard about it, he went down to the stronghold. Now the Philistines came and overran the Valley of Rephaim. So David inquired of the Lord, saying, "Shall I go up against the Philistines? Will You hand them over to me?" And the Lord said to David, "Go up, for I will certainly hand the Philistines over to you." Then David came to Baal-perazim and defeated them there; and he said, "The Lord has broken through my enemies before me like the breakthrough of waters." Therefore he named that place Baal-perazim. And the Philistines abandoned their idols there, so David and his men carried them away. Now the Philistines came up once again and overran the Valley of Rephaim. So David inquired of the Lord, but He said, "You shall not go directly up; circle around behind them and come at them in front of the baka-shrubs. And it shall be, when you hear the sound*

of marching in the tops of the baka-shrubs, then you shall act promptly, for then the Lord will have gone out before you to strike the army of the Philistines." Then David did so, just as the Lord had commanded him; he struck and killed the Philistines from Geba as far as Gezer. (2 Samuel 5:17–32)

David was in a situation in which he could have decided on his own about how to handle the Philistines. He could have listened to what anyone else had to say about the situation as well, such as war strategies, concerns and whether they should attack. But instead, David gleaned from the Lord's counsel, and, in turn, he was victorious. After his great victory, when the Philistines returned to the same spot, David could have just repeated what he had done before. But instead, he met with the Lord again so he could hear God's counsel for the current situation.

This is a prime example of "leaning not on your own understanding and trusting not in your own ways." (See Proverbs 3:5–6.) David knew that the Lord would have something different to say to him during the second time of counsel. If David had insisted on doing what he wanted to do or simply repeated the past counsel of the Lord, they would have been defeated. God can change His mind on a dime, watching to see how pliable you are and how well you listen. Obedience is inseparable from love. David's love for God was reflected in his desire to constantly seek God's perfect counsel.

The current counsel of God is necessary when shaking comes. In John 9, Jesus spits on the ground and makes mud to be applied to a blind man's eyes. Then He sends the man to be washed and healed. Never again does Jesus do this. In Mark 8, Jesus spat directly into a blind man's eyes and then laid hands on him for his healing to occur.

There are many displays of the gifts of the Spirit. I allow the spirit of counsel to speak to me while I am ministering, teaching or prophesying. It is key that we learn the spirit of counsel in ministry so that our decision making is directly from God. We must make sure that we are in tune with the spirit of counsel, which brings about the strategy of heaven, because He typically interweaves His divine message into His methods.

God does not merely give us an answer that will only help us in our present situation. He also sews prophetic revelation into the public display of why you are doing it the way He has directed. Everything God does is calculated, revelatory, prophetic, pointed and successful. This is another important reason why we must be in the spirit of counsel. There is prophetic revelation in it for yourself, for those around you and even for the generations that follow you. There is a prophetic message sewn into transition and method, from Moses to Joshua. When you look at the entirety of the Word of God, these are the only four people who, according to

God's perfect and supernatural counsel, had to cross bodies of water to implement God's plan. This was very calculated by sewing the prophetic realm of heaven into their strategies. Moses crossed the Red Sea supernaturally, and then, Joshua crossed the Jordan River supernaturally.

Elijah and Moses are the two witnesses in the book of Revelation. Many believe the witnesses to be Elijah and Enoch because they were caught up with the Lord, but from what I understand in the Bible, that does not add up, especially considering that it was Elijah and Moses who were at the mount of transfiguration.

Moses went up to Jordan and passed on the baton to Joshua. We are a representation of Joshua stepping into the promised land with God, while Moses was a forerunner. This is also seen in Revelation, just before the Lord's return. Crossing over bodies of water represents a transition point. Moses and Elijah were the top dogs of understanding supernatural provision.

And after the three and a half days, the breath of life from God came into them, and they stood on their feet; and great fear fell upon those who were watching them. And they heard a loud voice from heaven saying to them, "Come up here." And they went up into heaven in the cloud, and their enemies watched them. And at that time there was a great earthquake, and a tenth of the city fell; seven thou-

> *sand people were killed in the earthquake, and the rest were terrified and gave glory to the God of heaven. The second woe has passed; behold, the third woe is coming quickly. Then the seventh angel sounded; and there were loud voices in heaven, saying, "The kingdom of the world has become the kingdom of our Lord and of His Christ; and He will reign forever and ever." And the twenty-four elders, who sit on their thrones before God, fell on their faces and worshiped God, saying, "We give You thanks, Lord God, the Almighty, the One who is and who was, because You have taken Your great power and have begun to reign. And the nations were enraged, and Your wrath came, and the time came for the dead to be judged, and the time to reward Your bond-servants the prophets and the saints and those who fear Your name, the small and the great, and to destroy those who destroy the earth." (Revelation 11:11–18)*

The two witnesses represent the resurrection of Jesus. The witnesses are examples of God's divine counsel, setting up the end times with men who were once passing their authority over to others now passing it along to us. They come back to manifest God's great counsel. God laid hidden messages and meanings in His counseling and communication. The spirit of counsel is vital because you are now dealing with the precise strategy of heaven at any given moment. It still takes wisdom, understanding and knowledge, but counsel applied can be taken to a whole new level. In this last hour, we are going to need the bridal company working in the spirit of counsel as never before. New wineskins are now being created for the Lord to fill with His new wine. These wineskins can only be created by the spirit of counsel. In the last hour, there will be people asking why their old counsel no longer works, while disregarding the Lord's new wine of counsel.

The now strategy of Heaven in the spirit of counsel is important right now to be able to build according to the blueprint of God. Do not worry about who is saying what and why they are saying it. Rather, realize they are walking in their specific grace and assignment, or they may not be in the current counsel of the Lord at all. Be mindful that, sometimes, people can be dogmatic about counsel the Lord has for them specifically. I once spoke with a minister friend who had conflicting views with me on a topic, however, we were both operating in the Holy Spirit with a fulfilling, fruitful and anointed belief that supported our own God-ordained assignments. We had different beliefs because of different anointings. Do not be pressured into believing that someone else's anointed belief is meant for you. You do what the Lord is telling you to do and in His direction of how to do it, all within the parameters of the Bible. The counsel of God changes, so intimacy is vital in maintaining the current counsel of the Lord. As the bride of Christ, we should find comfort in Him and in what He has to say. Without the spirit of counsel, you cannot pick up on the shifts in His planning for the now season in which He is operating.

6
THE SPIRIT OF MIGHT

THE HEBREW DEFINITION of might is "strength, courage, power, ability, capacity for, and substance." You will often see a substance gift accompanying a revelatory gift. For instance, you often see words of wisdom accompanying healing. The doorway of healing illuminates faith, opening people to Him. The spirit of might drives these together: Wonderful Counselor and Mighty God. The spirit of might brings about tenacious courage, strength and boldness that is needed for the last hour. We are the Joshua company, prophetically carrying on from where Moses was left behind, and going into the promised land.

> *Be strong and courageous, for you shall give this people possession of the land which I swore to their fathers to give them. Only be strong and very cou-*

rageous; be careful to do according to all the Law which Moses My servant commanded you; do not turn from it to the right or to the left, so that you may achieve success wherever you go. This Book of the Law shall not depart from your mouth, but you shall meditate on it day and night, so that you may be careful to do according to all that is written in it; for then you will make your way prosperous, and then you will achieve success. Have I not commanded you? Be strong and courageous! Do not be terrified nor dismayed, for the Lord your God is with you wherever you go." (Joshua 1:6–9)

In these verses, the Lord is telling Joshua to display His creative, miraculous, healing and courageous power. I want to encourage some of you who feel timid or weak, not knowing how you will be in critical or trying times. The spirit of might will show up and supernaturally change you. The spirit of might does not rest on the proud but on the humble.

The spirit of might obliterates fear and timidity, not only in the face of persecution but also when you are obeying the Lord. You can have revelation but if you do not have might and courage, you will never be able to step out in that revelation. Many people fall because of their fear of failure. God may have spoken to you, but you also need the spirit of might to act boldly in what He has spoken to you. We need the spirit of might in the last hour as never before because persecution will be at an all-time high. This is not "doom and gloom." The last hour will be the most glorious time the church has ever seen. The spirit of might implements power and miracles, but it also implements strength, capability and triumph. The spirit of might on the church will be unshakeable when butted up against the world.

The Holy Spirit despises fear because it short circuits destiny. Fear is out to paralyze people. It will have you nervously pacing around the mountain you are meant to climb. If you can smell fear, turn away from it because it is not conducive of the presence of God.

Shadrach, Meshach, and Abed-nego replied to the king, "Nebuchadnezzar, we are not in need of an answer to give you concerning this matter. If it be so, our God whom we serve is able to rescue us from the furnace of blazing fire; and He will rescue us from your hand, O king. But even if He does not, let it be known to you, O king, that we are not going to serve your gods nor worship the golden statue that you have set up." (Daniel 3:16-18)

THE SPIRIT OF KNOWLEDGE

The Hebrew understanding of knowledge includes skill, truth, concern, comprehension, and expertise. The spirit of knowledge is the fullness of who God is in the matter. It is not limited to what we understand things to be in the natural. Remember that the spirit of knowledge was one of the spirits that was missing from the time of William Seymour.

The primitive root of the Hebrew word knowledge or to know is translated as "to be certain by seeing." The realm of seeing is going to be paramount in these last days. To see is to know in the spirit realm. I believe the seer realm is a major doorway that will unlock the spirit of knowledge in this last hour. Once this knowledge is unlocked, wisdom, understanding and counsel come into play. Knowledge must be in the equation for the math to add up. Without knowledge, counsel has nothing to strategize with, and wisdom and understanding have nothing to build from or stand between.

The seer realm is for all; we are all supposed to see into the spirit realm. The church of Laodicea, the last church in the book of Revelation, our generation, is told by Jesus to anoint their eyes so they may see. The spirit of knowledge was lacking in the last generation, but it will not lack in this generation. To see is to know, and then the rest of the seven spirits can be applied. Let's imagine that David did not know the Philistines were atop the mountain in 2 Samuel. David would never have had the wisdom and understanding to seek the counsel of the Lord. Knowledge is key to the entire list of seven spirits because without it there is no foundation.

For the Lord gives wisdom; from His mouth come knowledge and understanding. (Proverbs 2:6)

This verse shows us how important each of these spirits are to each other. They are foundational to each other in keeping God's Spirit and heart behind each of them. Without knowledge, there can be no wisdom or understanding. Without understanding, wisdom can become cruelty. Without wisdom, knowledge can become prideful.

There are many different areas in life in which knowledge is applicable. Knowing Him is knowing everlasting life. From there follows the knowledge of God's will, applied in all different areas of life. The Holy Spirit knows all things, bringing vision to people in the fog of confusion. We must sustain a deep knowing of Him.

Not everyone who says to Me, "Lord, Lord," will enter the kingdom of heaven, but the one who does the will of My Father who is in heaven will enter. Many will say to Me on that day, "Lord, Lord, did we not prophesy in Your name, and in Your name cast out demons, and in Your name perform many miracles?" And then I will declare to them, "I never knew you; leave Me, you who practice lawlessness." (Matthew 7:21–23)

> *Then the kingdom of heaven will be comparable to ten virgins, who took their lamps and went out to meet the groom. Five of them were foolish, and five were prudent. For when the foolish took their lamps, they did not take extra oil with them; but the prudent ones took oil in flasks with their lamps. Now while the groom was delaying, they all became drowsy and began to sleep. But at midnight there finally was a shout: "Behold, the groom! Come out to meet him." Then all those virgins got up and trimmed their lamps. But the foolish virgins said to the prudent ones, "Give us some of your oil, because our lamps are going out." However, the prudent ones answered, "No, there most certainly would not be enough for us and you too; go instead to the merchants and buy some for yourselves." But while they were on their way to buy the oil, the groom came, and those who were ready went in with him to the wedding feast; and the door was shut. Yet later, the other virgins also came, saying, "Lord, lord, open up for us." But he answered, "Truly I say to you, I do not know you." Be on the alert then, because you do not know the day nor the hour. (Matthew 25:1–13)*

There is an important difference in this verse having to do with knowing the Lord. In Matthew 7, Jesus said He never knew the many. In Matthew 25, the Bridegroom (Jesus) said He did not know them. The difference is that the Bridegroom, at some point, knew the Matthew 25 virgins, whereas He never knew the many. It is unreal to me that people who do miracles and display the wonderful power of God through their personal lives still do not know Him. Intimacy with the Lord is knowing Him, and this is key in maintaining the seven spirits.

Without a doubt, you will deal with opposition. The devil does not play fair and he will use anything he can against you. The spirit of knowledge will help you see through the schemes of the enemy. The knowledge that God has will save you from walking into traps or stepping on the enemy's landmines. The spirit of knowledge will reveal the location and source of your opposition.

You may know God's will, but if it is not aligned with the timing of God, you may not see it become relevant for a long time. There have been many times when God has spoken to me about something, but I did not see the fruition of His words for many years. The spirit of knowledge sees and knows the times and seasons. We may know the will of God but still not know His timing.

The spirit of knowledge provides the where and the who for your specific calling. Your calling cannot be implemented without the spirit of knowledge. How would you know where to go or what to do without the knowledge of the Lord? Target areas that the Lord targets. Jesus would only do what the Father was doing and say what the Father was saying. You can miss the fullness of your destiny by missing the where and the who for your specific calling.

The spirit of knowledge makes those things that were once obscure to be understood. He knows why ladybugs fly by you and why rain comes when it does. God has knowledge about even the simplest of things. He knows all things.

7
THE SPIRIT OF THE FEAR OF THE LORD

THE FEAR OF the Lord in Hebrew translates as "to reverence or to be in awe of." I would like to point out how clearly the knowledge and the fear of the Lord are coupled together throughout Scripture. Clearly, the fear of the Lord is the most important factor, second only to the Holy Spirit Himself. I am not trying to prioritize one spirit over the other because once one flame goes out, the rest go out or become unbalanced. We must have all seven.

But the fear of the Lord is so vital because of its substance. The fear of the Lord is the next in line on the menorah. It is the thread that keeps all seven in place. Have you ever had a sweater or blanket for which if you pulled on one loose thread, the entire thing would slowly and completely come apart? That thread is the fear of the Lord. If you tug on the fear of the Lord, all the others unravel. Without the fear of the Lord, we will get nowhere. And things are only going to become more heated in these last days. The fear of the Lord is an important asset within the nature of God that has been given to this last-hour bridal company.

> *The fear of the Lord is the beginning of knowledge; fools despise wisdom and instruction. (Proverbs 1:7)*

> *Because they hated knowledge and did not choose the fear of the Lord. (Proverbs 1:29)*

> *The fear of the Lord is the beginning of wisdom, and the knowledge of the Holy One is understanding. (Proverbs 9:10)*

> *And to mankind He said, "Behold, the fear of the Lord, that is wisdom; and to turn away from evil is understanding." (Job 28:28)*

We see, in Proverbs 1:7, that knowledge, instruction and wisdom are in tandem with the fear of the Lord. It is the anchor that holds these other attributes of the Lord in place.

The seven spirits are sewn deeply into the fear of the Lord. After Solomon wrote twelve chapters of Ecclesiastes, a book about how everything is vanity, he concluded with this verse:

The conclusion, when everything has been heard, is: fear God and keep His commandments, because this applies to every person. For God will bring every act to judgment, everything which is hidden, whether it is good or evil. (Ecclesiastes 12:13–14)

This verse can be easily boiled down very simply: fear God and keep His commandments. It is not just a good idea; it also is the substance of who the Lord is. It is the Spirit of God, not just a reverential take on the Lord. It is a part of the fullness of God. I believe we will see it increase in the true company as we move closer to the last hour.

In the last days we will begin to see a great falling away, people following myths and false teachings that tickle their ears rather than believing in the truth of the Word. People will lose their fear of the Lord. To those who have the fear of the Lord, the last days will be great and wonderful, but for those who do not, it will be dreadful. Both are the fear of the Lord but for different reasons. We need the fear of the Lord back in the church.

God is not our sugar daddy, homeboy or sidekick. He is the Lord God Almighty, King of the universe. He is Lord over all. The elders throw their crowns down at Him. Abba Father is healthy, but so is the fear and reverence of our Lord. He is enthroned. If He moves even a pinky, it affects the entire universe. The highest heavens cannot contain Him. We need a return of reverence to bring balance to the church. This does not mean we are not godly enough to enter into the throne room or that He is not our loving Father, but irreverence is a dangerous place to be. This is not anger, judgment or meant to scare you. It is meant to bring honor and reverence. You see John the beloved place his head on the chest of Jesus on earth but then fall at His feet once in the realm of glory. The fear of the Lord is all over the Word of God, It is very biblical.

> *For if we go on sinning willfully after receiving the knowledge of the truth, there no longer remains a sacrifice for sins, but a terrifying expectation of judgment and the fury of a fire which will consume the adversaries. Anyone who has ignored the Law of Moses is put to death without mercy on the testimony of two or three witnesses.*
>
> *How much more severe punishment do you think he will deserve who has trampled underfoot the Son of God, and has regarded as unclean the blood of the covenant by which he was sanctified, and has insulted the Spirit of grace? For we know Him who said, "Vengeance is Mine, I will repay." And again, "The Lord will judge His people." It is a terrifying thing to fall into the hands of the living God. (Hebrews 10: 26–31)*

And I looked when He broke the sixth seal, and there was a great earthquake; and the sun became as black as sackcloth made of hair, and the whole moon became like blood; and the stars of the sky fell to the earth, as a fig tree drops its unripe figs when shaken by a great wind. The sky was split apart like a scroll when it is rolled up, and every mountain and island was removed from its place. Then the kings of the earth and the eminent people, and the commanders and the wealthy and the strong, and every slave and free person hid themselves in the caves and among the rocks of the mountains; and they said to the mountains and the rocks, "Fall on us and hide us from the sight of Him who sits on the throne, and from the wrath of the Lamb; for the great day of Their wrath has come, and who is able to stand?" (Revelation 6:12–17)

These verses display a side of the Lord that I believe we will begin to see more and more as we get closer to the great and terrible day of the Lord. Even in what some will see as God being terrible, He will still be in His perfect love. Regardless of what you believe is His true perfect love, it will still come. The fear of the Lord will have its way no matter what. Reverential fear of the Lord is viewed negatively but when we get too top heavy in "love language" and forget the fear of the Lord, we can slip into irreverence. Fear of the Lord interweaves into the seven spirits in a deep and intimate way. Also, the fear of the Lord is what will sustain and stabilize you in times of persecution, trial and pressure. That is why it is vital in these last hours. When the fear of the Lord burns brightly, it will consume all other fears.

> *And do not be afraid of those who kill the body but are unable to kill the soul; but rather fear Him who is able to destroy both soul and body in hell. (Matthew 10:28)*

When the fear of the Lord is burning at full brightness, it dominates and minimizes all other fears. When you fear nothing but God, you can walk successfully with your focus on Him.

I had a dream at the end of a Daniel fast, a typical occurrence when finishing fasts. Fasting opens you to the wider spiritual realm, allowing for more experiences to occur. If you are ever stirring up darkness, it is because you are furthering destiny with God. In my dream, I saw four different beings that I knew were from the dark realm. They made me think they were like the four living creatures of Revelation 4, but from the dark side and not of God. In the dream, I saw them looking for me. Interestingly, I was watching them from the perspective of my son, not from my own perspective. I was watching them through my son. As I watched them look for me, one of them disappeared and then reappeared behind me, breathing down my neck. It wanted to persecute me to death. But amazingly, the fear of the Lord was so strong that there was no fear of the creature in my son. I could feel the fear of the Lord even after waking from the dream. The spirit of the fear of the Lord was so strong that even high-ranking members of hell could not bring fear to me or my son.

The pressures of the world and the dark realm will be ever increasing in the last days, so we must hold tightly to our reverence for God. The fear of the Lord is so real and tangible that the fears of the world will not be able to interrupt our reverence for Him.

If you have the fear of man, you will always find yourself submitting to the approval of man. If there is fear of man present in your life, it is because the fear of God is not burning at full capacity in your life. The fear of the Lord takes all of life and puts it in perfect alignment with Him. If you revere sickness to a high degree, then you will submit to every appearance of sickness. High levels of fear turn into big life changes that God does not want you to make. If you are changing your lifestyle because of the fear you have, you will become subject to it. You will always submit to that for which you have reverence—good or bad. Fear is fear, whether healthy (for God) or not (for anything else). If we are honest, many of us still carry fears that need to be replaced with the fear of God. Fear is rampant in this hour. Live out of the Word of God and the fullness of the cross. Quickly turn from anything that is contradicting the Word, so you do not yield to it. So many people are fearing sickness when they should be fearing the Lord. You empower that which you fear, so fear the Lord. Do not become vulnerable to fears of the world.

We need the fear of the Lord to start crushing other fears and reverances. The spirit of the fear of the Lord will obliterate all other reverences and annihilate all other fears. Here are important verses on the fear of the Lord:

Let all the earth fear the Lord; let all the inhabitants of the world stand in awe of Him. (Psalm 33:8)

The fear of the Lord is a fountain of life, by which one may avoid the snares of death. (Proverbs 14:27)

Fear the Lord, you His saints; for to those who fear Him there is no lack of anything. (Psalm 34:9)

Blessed is a person who fears the Lord, who greatly delights in His commandments. (Psalm 112:1)

The reward of humility and the fear of the Lord are riches, honor, and life. (Proverbs 22:4)

Therefore, having these promises, beloved, let's cleanse ourselves from all defilement of flesh and spirit, perfecting holiness in the fear of God. (2 Corinthians 7:1)

Honor all people, love the brotherhood, fear God, honor the king. (1 Peter 2:17)

By mercy and truth atonement is made for wrongdoing, and by the fear of the Lord one keeps away from evil. (Proverbs 16:6)

So the church throughout Judea, Galilee, and Samaria enjoyed peace, as it was being built up; and as it continued in the fear of the Lord and in the comfort of the Holy Spirit, it kept increasing. (Acts 9:31)

That which you fear will overtake you. The reverence you give something automatically empowers it into a leadership role over your life. We do not want the focus of our prayers to be about getting out of our problems and fears but to be about striving for a closer intimacy with God.

We want to be in a company in which the fear of the Lord is foundational. You can see people and churches whose foundations do not have the fear of the Lord. It will only be a matter of time before their eternal fruit in heaven withers, they tumble, and are burned up on the day of judgment. God's people are built up by walking in the fear of Him.

The seven spirits of the Lord are for us today. They are needed as we confront the end times. The Lord desires that we all work through the seven spirits, maintaining them through intimacy, as the menorah exemplifies. Each spirit is purposeful, necessary and reliant on other spirits so that we may obtain them all in balanced form.

The spirit of wisdom is so we may judge rightly in matters relating to life and conduct. The spirit of understanding is so that we may stand under the Lord and His perfect will. The spirit of counsel is so that we can glean from the Lord's consultation. The spirit of might is the substance of courage and strength the Lord gives so that we may endure. The spirit of knowledge allows us to know of the goodness of God by seeing it. Live a life that intentionally chooses to follow the seven spirits so that you maintain balance in your relationship with Him.

BRIAN GUERIN is the founding president of Bridal Glory International. He graduated from the Brownsville School of Ministry/F.I.R.E. in 2001, and now travels throughout the U.S. and the world teaching and preaching the gospel of the Lord Jesus Christ. Brian has appeared on T.B.N. and GOD-TV and currently hosts his own broadcasting channel on YouTube. He also authored two previously released books, *Modern Day Mysticism* and *God of Wonders*. His main passion and emphasis in life is to draw the Bride of Christ into greater intimacy with the Bridegroom Himself-Jesus Christ, leading to the maturity of the Bride and the culmination of His glorious return. Brian also enjoys bringing great emphasis and depth to the art of hearing the voice of God through dreams, visions, signs, and wonders.

VISIT BRIDAL GLORY ON THE WEB & SOCIAL:
WWW.BRIDALGLORY.COM

SOCIAL: *@BRIDALGLORY*

FREE EXCERPT FROM

To Know Him

**available at
amazon**

I
THE DIVINE DOOR

I GAVE MY life to the Lord in 1998, and as I have grown in my walk with God since then, it has become solidified in me that the ultimate goal and purpose in life is *to know Him*. That's what this book is about, merging the Spirit and Word in such a way that we see life purely through this lens. The more I walk with Jesus year in and year out, I go deeper into the realization that *knowing Him* is the greatest mission, objective, and destination you can find yourself in search of. *Knowing Him* is a never-ending journey of discovery. Once we discover our destination, it is the best place we can be in pursuit of—day in and day out.

As we go through learning about what it means to *know Him,* keep an image of a beautiful *door* in front of you. Jesus almost always mentions a *door* when describing the intimacy of *knowing Him* in Scripture. *To know*

Him is the greatest *doorway* to walk towards and be continually stepping through. This *doorway* is where you want every fiber of life to be heading towards and funneling through. The end result of all of life's desires is this beautiful *doorway* of *knowing Him*. Solomon

We see in Revelation that Jesus knocks on a *doorway* to enter so that we may dine with Him. "Behold, I stand at the *door* and knock. If anyone hears My voice and opens the door, I will come in to him and dine with him, and he with Me" (Revelation 3:20).

Often in Scripture we see that there is a *door* connected with entering into *knowing Him*. In Matthew 25 we read of more *doorway* imagery in the Parable of the Wise and Foolish Virgins:

> *"And while they went to buy, the bridegroom came, and those who were ready went in with him to the wedding; and the door was shut. Afterward the other virgins came also, saying, 'Lord, Lord, open to us!' But he answered and said, 'Assuredly, I say to you, I do not know you.'" (Matthew 25:10-12)*

We read that the five wise virgins had enough oil in their lamps to step through the *doorway* into the wedding feast with Him. Right before the wise virgins enter in, the five foolish virgins try bartering oil from them. *Those who were ready,* the five wise virgins, enter through the *door*. But the five foolish virgins are shut out from entering the intimate feast with the Bridegroom.

Doorway imagery is also used for intimacy in prayer, "But you, when you pray, go into your room, and when you have shut your *door*, pray to your Father who is in the secret place" (Matthew 6:6). When we go into prayer we close ourselves in with Christ and out from the rest of the world.

Jesus uses the *doorway* imagery again when describing Himself, "Then Jesus said to them again, 'Most assuredly, I say to you, I am the door of the sheep' " (John 10:7). How beautiful is it then that a *doorway* is the image that Christ uses to not only describe Himself but also to describe deep intimacy with Him?

The *doorway* is the purpose or intentions of our hearts. The desires and depths of who we are, or the reasons why we do the things we do, determine what *doorway* we are going through or seeking to discover. When we go through the core motives of our hearts and start recognizing why we pursue Christ, we may come to the realization that we are missing the mark. The highest standard by which Jesus gauges at the end is whether or not we *know Him*. May we always be evolving into fresh desire with our hearts to be searching for this *door*. *Knowing Him* trumps everything, and from that intimacy comes the gifts of the Spirit, success, fulfillment of destiny, and the Great Commission. Through understanding the importance of *knowing*

Him, let us recalibrate our pursuit as individuals and as the Church.

Many people have connected; to be near God is to be blessed. For instance, The ark of the covenant was left at Obed-Edom's house in 2 Samuel. *"The ark of the Lord remained in the house of Obed-Edom the Gittite three months. And the Lord blessed Obed-Edom and all his household" (2 Samuel 6:11).* For the three months that he was in the tangible presence of God, everything around him was prosperous. He was blessed beyond measure because he was in the proximity of God. But this was only after the ark of the covenant was brought into his home through his *doorway*. We often confuse the blessing of God with being near to Him; therefore, we strive for blessings rather than Christ Himself. But only when we open our hearts to God will His blessings become evident to us.

Other motives, if put before the doorway of *knowing Him,* become the true reason or initial door by which our life is being funneled through. And if we are not careful, we begin to make decisions from our deepest desires within. Far too often we believe we have already entered into the doorway of *knowing Him*, but we do not have deep relationship or intimacy with Christ. Sadly, what is driving a lot of people or pulling them out of bed in the morning is the desire to be successful in business or ministry.

We neglect *knowing Him* when we only desire education, impact, platform, fame, or success. These are all to be mere additions in the impact of your life's pursuit of Him. There are people with doctorates or PhDs behind their name that know far more than I do from a scriptural perspective, but yet, they cannot hear the voice of God. They have no emotional connection or relationship with Him. Similarly, Orthodox Jews know the Old Testament better than any other; some even have entire books of the Old Testament memorized. But in the New Testament Jesus approaches their understanding and says *the Scriptures speak of me*. Orthodox Jews often *think* they know God better than anyone else and we can be just as sure in spite of not truly *knowing Him*. I want to know God and the reasons why He says what He says, not just Scriptures and concepts to impress others. When this *doorway* is set before you and is all you are in search of, then the praises or opposition of men become irrelevant.

As soon as the *doorway* is not first and foremost for what we are trying to accomplish, then everything will fall out of place. The value of what you do on any given day is to *know Him*. And when we *know Him*, He will lovingly sift through our hearts and lead us back to Him.

When God observes our hearts, He can recognize why we get up in the morning. Is it for Him or our own desires? To *know Him,* to walk through His metaphorical *door*, is the most important thing we could do. To have a cup of coffee with Jesus, so to speak, stare deep into His eyes, and truly *know Him*. To feel Him closer than anyone else you think you deeply know. That is what walking through the *doorway* looks like. Our ultimate goal in life is to walk through the doorway of intimacy and to fulfill what He asks of us.

In this process God will reveal our ulterior motives, even if in the name of Jesus. This revelation is so that we may begin to move from other motives and into the *doorway* of *knowing Him*, but only when we are standing directly before the Lord. His true sifting fire will burn the chaff and He will leave with gold, silver, and precious stones. And the only thing that produces the gold, silver, and precious stones is walking through the *door of knowing Him*.

> *"And this is eternal life, that they may know You, the only true God, and Jesus Christ whom You have sent."* (John 17:3)

We often confuse the blessing of God with being near to Him; therefore, we strive for blessings rather than Christ Himself. It is when we open our hearts to God that His blessings will become evident to us. This is the overriding gemstone of life. Only after walking through His *doorway* can we truly love our spouse, our family, our neighbor, and be like the image of Christ. We strive to become those who are so truly infatuated and lost in love with Jesus that everything they do is caught in unity with Him.

> *"Jesus said to him, 'I am the way, the truth, and the life. No one comes to the Father except through Me. If you had known Me, you would have known My Father also; and from now on you know Him and have seen Him.'" (John 14:6-7)*

Jesus says here that if we know the Father, then we must know Him. We see Him using the filter that He sees everyone through: Do they know Me? He does not look at them through the filter of how incredible they may be or what they do or do not do. He simply sees those who are in front of Him and asks, *"Do they know Me?"* In no way should this bring condemnation. In the truthful love of God our hearts will be enlightened. Jesus uses this lens again here, "Then they said to Him, 'Where is Your Father?' Jesus answered, 'You know neither Me nor My Father. If you had known Me, you would have known My Father also'" (John 8:19). He is essentially telling those He was speaking to, "If you would walk through My doorway, you would know My Father."

We see the gauge of knowing God in the Old Testament as well, "Now the sons of Eli were *worthless*, and they did not know the Lord" (1 Samuel 2:12). They were worthless not because of a standard they were not living up to or because they were not knowledgeable enough on the Scriptures. There was a lack of value on these men because they did not know the Lord. The most valuable people on the earth are those who authentically *know Him*. Not the powerful, gifted, or successful. Although those attributes are good and in God's will, they should not be our priority. In Matthew 7 we read about preachers functioning in the gifts, evangelizing, and healing the sick, but they still did not *know Him*. At the end of our time on earth Jesus will gauge us by whether or not we *know Him* and nothing else. All of creation was made to know and love Him.

2
INTIMACY'S VALUE

"I am the good shepherd; and I know My sheep, and am known by My own. As the Father knows Me, even so I know the Father; and I lay down My life for the sheep." (John 10:14-15)

TIME AND AGAIN we see Jesus putting value on knowing Him intimately. You can see the constant value and qualifying standard Jesus and the Word put on knowing Him. This quantifying standard in life is gauged similarly to how we place value on what we are connected to. We connect ourselves to many things whether we pay attention to them or not.

We connect to and place value on all things imaginable. For instance, in construction, if you want hardwood floors that are really strong, you need the right type of wood. You pay attention to the caliber of the wood, how tight the grains are, and its density. There is a value standard that you put on building hardwood floors, just like you would put on everything else in life. The things you like: cars, instruments, technology, whatever it may be, has a value system on them that determines how much interest you have in them. Those interests will only be as valuable as the level at which you gauge their worth. Our lives will be value-gauged by Jesus, down to the very end of our time on earth, and that gauge is whether or not we *know Him*. Not how gifted you are, or how many followers you have, or churches you planted; it comes down to one thing: *did you know Him or not?*

The tape breaks in the race of life, *whether we know Him or not*. This is the treasure chest where the "X" is marked out for the exact design within what we call humanity. *Knowing Him*. This is the victorious finish line, as mentioned. *Knowing Him*. This is the most valuable fortune or pearl you will ever find hidden in the field of life. *Knowing Him*. Start paying attention to the value and ultimate finish line type of qualities Jesus puts on *knowing Him*.

At times we are not careful of our motivations and need to reassess aspects of our life, like prayer and Bible reading. Far too often, if we were honest before the Lord, we would see how many different things are driving us to Him. If we allow multiple things to drive us to Him, then we lower our gauge of *knowing Him*. It is dangerously easy to fall into the trap of having a low value on intimacy with Christ. I have seen it in my own life and others that have been "walking with the Lord" but lack a deep intimacy with Jesus.

Our end goal should be to not only become like Him, to do tasks for Him, or to win and overcome through Him. While all of these are clearly wrapped up in His will and desire for our lives, it is the ultimate doorway of *knowing Him* that is our end goal. I have heard the focal point of reflecting the image of God so heavily preached that we can miss the intimate relationship of Jesus in our lives. To *know Him* is to be *like Him*. Often, the message of being the image of Christ is prioritized in our vision so largely that we miss Him moving to our left and right. Only from *knowing Him* will we most reflect Him and His image.

> *"Now by this we know that we know Him, if we keep His commandments. He who says, 'I know Him,' and does not keep His commandments, is a liar, and the truth is not in him." (1 John 2:3-4)*

It is not only Jesus that describes intimacy with Him as *knowing Him*. You can see John telling us that the *door* is what we must be in pursuit of to have access to the pinnacle of life. *Knowing Him* or stepping into *His doorway* will be evident through whether or not we keep His commandments. To be in pursuit of *only* keeping His commandments misses the entire purpose of keeping them. We must *know Him* to *keep them*.

> *"Yes, everything else is worthless when compared with the infinite value of knowing Christ Jesus my Lord. For his sake I have discarded everything else, counting it all as garbage, so that I could gain Christ and become one with him. I no longer count on my own righteousness through obeying the law; rather, I become righteous through faith in Christ. For God's way of making us right with himself depends on faith. I want to know Christ and experience the mighty power that raised him from the dead. I want to suffer with him, sharing in his death." (Philippians 3:8-10, NLT)*

Paul sums up the idea of *knowing Him*. He tells us *for his sake* everything else pales in comparison to *intimacy with Him*. We could never put a price on such infinite value of what we gain in Christ. Knowing Him is unmatched in comparison to knowing anything or anyone else. We must count everything else in life as garbage so that we may gain Christ and become *one with Him*. Paul is telling us he would get rid of everything in His life, disregarding it all as long as he can step through the *door of intimacy with Jesus*.

Paul then starts expressing the supporting factors that come from *knowing Him*. He tells us his righteousness is not from obeying the law, but from faith in Christ alone. He then explains that we are made right by our faith in Him and through Him. Every good thing that God has us do is funneled through *knowing Him*, and Paul tells us multiple times in this beautiful passage. The call to know Jesus is a thread that is sewn throughout the entirety of the New Testament. At the end of the passage we see Paul desperately wanting to become so intimate with Jesus that he experiences the power of the resurrection. Through this door of *knowing Him* comes the power of the resurrection. I have righteousness not in myself alone. From *knowing Him*, may the power of His resurrection share with me His sufferings, that I may become like Him in His death.

The ulterior motives of life, the selfish ambitions, cannot hold on to you when your sole desire is to please God. When you are madly in love with Jesus, all you care about is getting before Him and hearing Him say *well done*. When in this place you are clicking into perfect sync with what God has always intended for you. The noise and the currents of the world disappear when you walk through *His door*. There is stillness in His presence, similar to being in the eye of a storm; everything is noisy or loud and distracting, but the stillness in His intimacy is life changing.

3
EXPERIENTIAL KNOWLEDGE

BOB JONES HAD an encounter with God where he died and was transported to heaven. During the encounter, God was asking Bob and others that were there, *"Did you learn to love?"* After many years of recognizing the prophetic, we must look at the inspiration or context behind the prophecies or spiritual events. When we do we reveal what God is trying to produce through us. Bob Jones' encounter with God revealed His intention, that He would send Bob back to earth to kickstart a *billion soul harvest*. Bob was open to the backdrop of God's intention: getting a prophet to birth revival in the nations.

Prophetic encounters should always point God's love back to earth. Through *knowing* God, His will is revealed to us. We see this here, "Seek the Kingdom of God above all else, and live righteously, and he will give you everything you need" (Matthew 6:33, NLT). When we walk through *His door*, God takes care of all of our needs. It is a provisional unlocking of heaven.

> *"Not everyone who says to Me, 'Lord, Lord,' shall enter the kingdom of heaven, but he who does the will of My Father in heaven. Many will say to Me in that day, 'Lord, Lord, have we not prophesied in Your name, cast out demons in Your name, and done many wonders in Your name? And then I will declare to them, 'I never knew you; depart from Me, you who practice lawlessness!'" (Matthew 7:21-23)*

Again here we see Jesus looking at us through the lense of knowing Him. The *many* in this verse were using their prophecies, encounters, and wonders as credibility of their spirituality. We read in Revelation that God is a rewarder of all of these actions. But they must be done through the *door of knowing Him.* We have to be very careful when we place our salvation on our actions and not on intimacy with Jesus.

After I found Christ when I was twenty years old, I saw an old friend that I was worldly with. He knew I had given my life to the Lord, and when I approached him, he hid the beer that he was holding behind him. As we talked he became very adamant that he was also a Christian. Unfortunately, from knowing his lifestyle, he was not in intimacy with Jesus. Likewise there are many professed Christians that stand on their actions as credibility for intimacy. From intimacy and *knowing Him* our actions will align with His will.

"As His divine power has given to us all things that pertain to life and godliness, through the knowledge of Him who called us by glory and virtue, by which have been given to us exceedingly great and precious promises, that through these you may be partakers of the divine nature, having escaped the corruption that is in the world through lust." (2 Peter 1:3-4)

Peter is making some high concept points of becoming like Him in this important verse. He is explaining going into eternal life, sharing in His sufferings, escaping corruption or human desires, and sharing in His divine nature. But Peter is still channeling all of this back *through the door of Him.* God has given us everything we need to live a godly life and we receive those tools through *knowing Him.*

The experiential working of His marvelous excellence is triggered by *knowing Him.* His great and precious promises are accessed through *knowing Him.* We share in His divine nature and become like Him by coming to *know Him.* You can escape the world's corruption caused by human desires by coming to *know Him. Knowing Him* is the primary factor in which everything swings to or from Him.

> *"[I] do not cease to give thanks for you, making mention of you in my prayers: that the God of our Lord Jesus Christ, the Father of glory, may give to you the spirit of wisdom and revelation in the knowledge of Him, the eyes of your understanding being enlightened; that you may know what is the hope of His calling, what are the riches of the glory of His inheritance in the saints, and what is the exceeding greatness of His power toward us who believe, according to the working of His mighty power which He worked in Christ when He raised Him from the dead and seated Him at His right hand in the heavenly places, far above all principality and power and might and dominion, and every name that is named, not only in this age but also in that which is to come." (Ephesians 1:16-21)*

Authors of the New Testament use *knowing Him* as an entrance point for healing, prophecy, teaching, and evangelism. Wisdom and revelation are important to fulfilling destiny and walking through our Christian lives. According to the apostle Paul, how do we receive the spirit of wisdom and revelation? Through the *knowledge of Him*. It is through this seed of knowledge that the fruit of the Spirit is produced in us.

A byproduct of *knowing Him* is having the eyes to your heart enlightened. When we have the knowledge of Him, the Great Commission will fall in place, we will heal the sick, and we will preach the Gospel. Knowing Jesus is the climax of everything we long for in Christ. The goal of gaining the righteousness of Christ is connected to this *door*. It is *knowing Him* that the hope to which you are called and the riches of His glorious inheritance for the saints is revealed. Walking through His door will give knowledge of His immeasurable greatness and power.

ETYMOLOGY OF KNOWING

All three passages that we have gone over, Ephesians 1:16-21, 2 Peter 1:3-4, and Philippians 3:8-10, all use the same root word for *knowing*. The Greek word for the *knowledge of Him* is translated back to *epignosis,* which has three separate definitions. One definition of *epignosis* is: *knowledge gained through firsthand relationships.* Secondhand knowledge is important and useful for the Kingdom of God, but firsthand relationship with God trumps all other forms of gaining knowledge. When we sit at the feet of Jesus and directly learn from our relationship with Him, we receive divine understanding. Our firsthand understanding comes from nowhere or no one but Christ alone.

The second definition of *epignosis* can be described as *contact knowledge.* We gain the knowledge of Him from being close to Him. The Bible is our direct contact with Jesus. It is tangible and available to us at all times. It is through our contact that understanding can be given to us directly from His hands. How much better is it to be in His doorway and receiving from His presence than to be waiting outside the doorway, trying to learn of Him from secondhand sources?

The third definition of *epignosis* is *to experientially know*. This is the knowledge that the authors of the New Testament are all talking about when using the term *knowing Him*. None of this involves heavy intellect, although that has its time and place, it doesn't take a group of theologians to determine the validity of the knowledge of Christ through experience. The New Testament authors are talking about firsthand relationship, not secondhand relational knowledge.

> *"That which was from the beginning, which we have heard, which we have seen with our eyes, which we have looked upon, and our hands have handled, concerning the Word of life." (1 John 1:1)*

John is telling us that He is bringing us the Word of life. He who existed from the beginning, whom he saw with his own eyes. He heard, felt, and saw the Lord firsthand, and to experience the Lord in that way you must be close to Him. Otherwise, when you experience Him through someone else, you are not exposed to the intimacy Christ has for you. When Paul, Peter, and others are telling us how to know God, they are referencing experience, hearing, seeing, and feeling Jesus.

NOTES